43721  SMITH ELEM. SCHOOL LIBRARY
99-50586

D1190246

## DATE DUE

940.54   Daily, Robert.
D
         The code talkers

DISCARD

# THE CODE
# TALKERS

# THE CODE TALKERS

## AMERICAN INDIANS IN WORLD WAR II

### BY ROBERT DAILY

A First Book
**Franklin Watts**
New York / Chicago / London / Toronto / Sydney

*To Debbie and Grant*

Cover art by Jane Sterrett

Photographs copyright ©: New York Public Library, Picture Collection: p. 2; The National Archives: pp. 8, 10, 35, 37, 39, 44, 46; Oklahoma Historical Society, Archives and Manuscripts Division: p. 12; Wide World Photos: pp. 16, 45, 54, 58; Archive Photos: pp. 18 (Herbert), 28, 30; Museum of Northern Arizona, Philip Johnston Collection #69.599: p. 20; UPI/Bettmann: pp. 22, 25, 27, 41, 51; The Bettmann Archive: p. 33; Kenji Kawano: pp. 55, 57.

Library of Congress Cataloging-in-Publication Data

Daily, Robert.
    The code talkers : American Indians in World War II / by Robert
    Daily.
            p. cm. — (A first book)
        Includes bibliographical references and index.
        ISBN 0-531-20190-2 (lib. bdg.)
            1. World War, 1939–1945—Cryptography—Juvenile literature.
        2. World War, 1939–1945—Participation, Indian—Juvenile literature.
        3. United States—Armed Forces—Indian troops—History—Juvenile
        literature. [1. World War, 1939–1945—Participation, Indian. 2. Cryptography.
        3. Navajo Indians. 4. Indians of North America.] I. Title. II. Series.
D810.C88D35 1995
940.54'8673—dc20                                                    94-41766
                                                                         CIP
                                                                          AC

Copyright © 1995 by Robert Daily
All rights reserved
Printed in the United States of America
6 5 4 3 2 1

# CONTENTS

# 1 THEIR WEAPONS WERE WORDS

The island of Saipan, a small speck in the middle of the Pacific Ocean, was no place to fight a war. The landscape was very rugged, with deep canyons and steep mountains. The vegetation was so thick that soldiers had to hack a path with their knives. In other words, there were countless places on Saipan for enemy soldiers to hide—and, it seemed, no way for American soldiers to locate their own comrades. Danger lurked behind every tree.

Early one morning in the summer of 1944, a battalion of U.S. Marines crawled through this wild terrain. Suddenly, an explosion rocked the ground! Dirt flew through the air as the soldiers ducked for cover.

The shots were coming not from the enemy—the Japanese soldiers ahead—but from American guns

The Navajo Code Talkers traveled a long, long way to defend their country in World War II. The mountains of the South Pacific islands were a far cry from the flat, dry deserts they called home.

behind. The marines had advanced to an area held by the Japanese only a few hours earlier. American gunners thought their artillery shells were aimed at the enemy. In fact, they were shelling their own troops. (Soldiers today call this "friendly fire," though it's anything but friendly.)

A marine on the front line grabbed a radio and shouted a message back to headquarters (HQ): "Hold your fire!" It was no use. All night long, Japanese soldiers who could speak perfect English had been sending phony radio messages to confuse the Americans. Did headquarters believe this marine's message was just another fake? Apparently so. Another shell exploded, this one landing even closer to the Americans. Again a marine got on the radio and begged the gunners at HQ to stop shooting. This time they answered with a request of their own.

"Do you have a Navajo?"

Quickly a Navajo Indian soldier was rushed to the radio. Speaking in his native language, he sent the same message—"Hold your fire!"—to a Navajo on the other end, who translated the tongue-twisting sounds back to English. This time, the officers at HQ knew the warning was real; there was no way the Japanese could have sent *that* message. The gunners changed the direction of their fire, saving many American lives. Once again, the Code Talkers had saved the day.

Dramatic scenes like this one were repeated throughout World War II. More than four hundred Code Talkers served their country in this bloody war, fighting in Europe and on Pacific islands from Guadalcanal to Iwo Jima. They sent messages from foxholes on beaches and from

Navajo cousins Preston and Frank Toledo relay a message in their native tongue. As you can see, the radios they used were not very portable!

trenches dug deep in dense jungles. They did their work with bullets whistling overhead and bombs bursting in air. These brave men—and, in many cases, teenage boys—fought a war of words. Their weapons were their native tongues.

Who were the Code Talkers? They were American Indians—men of the Navajo, Choctaw, Comanche, Creek, Ojibwa, Menominee, and Hopi tribes—who used their languages to code and decode messages in the heat of battle. They spoke both everyday words and hundreds of special code words. Because the enemy was not familiar with either the language *or* the code, they could not decipher these vital messages. This gave American forces a big advantage in battle.

Throughout history, it has been essential for armies to keep messages secret. If your enemies intercept your messages, they can learn many things about you—how many soldiers you have, where they are located, when you plan to attack. And if they know these things, they can counter whatever is coming their way. For this reason, armies disguise their messages in various codes, symbols (sometimes letters) that represent secret meanings.

In centuries past, armies have tried sending messages in languages that were unknown to the enemy. But few have been as successful as the Code Talkers. During World War II, the Japanese were able to crack most of the American codes—but they never could decipher the Navajo language. In fact, some experts have credited the Navajos with creating "the world's most unbreakable code."

Joseph Oklahombi, a Choctaw Code Talker, was decorated for his service in World War I. The Choctaws were the originators of Code Talking.

The Navajo have gotten credit as the first American Indians to use their native tongue in battle. The very first Code Talkers, however, were Choctaws serving in World War I.

The year was 1918. The scene was the dense woods of northern France. German soldiers had pushed into France and taken a position in an area called Forest Ferme. The Americans knew that a surprise attack would be the best way to drive the Germans back. Unfortunately, the Germans had gotten very good at listening to, and decoding, American radio messages. If they could do that, they would always be ready to counter the American attacks.

One night an American captain was walking among his troops when he heard some Choctaw soldiers speaking their language. He was baffled by these strange sounds—and figured the Germans would be just as confused. The captain found fourteen Choctaws in Company E of the 142nd Infantry and recruited them as radio communicators.

On October 27, 1918, when American soldiers attacked the Germans at Forest Ferme, they found telephone lines that had been abandoned by the enemy. A Choctaw would use these lines to send messages in his native tongue; at the other end another Choctaw would translate the message back to English. The Germans were listening in, but they were completely baffled by these tongue-twisting sounds. They never knew what hit them, and within three days they were in full retreat. The commanding officer later said, "The enemy's complete surprise is evidence that he could not decipher the messages."

During their service in France, the Choctaws developed military terms that didn't appear in their language. A piece of artillery, for example, was called a "big gun." A machine gun was "little gun shoot fast." Battalions were designated by one, two, or three grains of corn.

The Choctaws received little publicity for their service in World War I, but they deserve a place in military history as the originators of Code Talking.

# 2 THE WAR BEGINS

On the morning of December 7, 1941, hundreds of Japanese airplanes roared across the Pacific Ocean and made a surprise raid on the U.S. naval base at Pearl Harbor, Hawaii. American planes and ships were bombed; hundreds of lives were lost. This dastardly attack immediately drew the United States into World War II.

The next day, the superintendent of the Navajo reservation in northeastern Arizona looked out his office window and saw a crowd of young men. They carried clothing, wrapped in red bandannas, and hunting rifles. When the superintendent asked what they were doing, one Navajo answered: "We're going to fight."

Actually, the *Dine*—loosely translated as "The People"—had expressed their readiness to fight long

The Navajos worked out their problems at tribal
council meetings, like this one at Window Rock,
Arizona. At one such meeting they pledged to
defend the United States in case of war.

before Pearl Harbor. In 1940, while war raged in Europe, the Navajo Tribal Council passed a resolution saying they stood ready "to aid and defend our Government and its institutions against all . . . armed conflict." The Navajo resolution proudly proclaimed that "there exists no purer concentration of Americanism than among the First Americans."

It was surprising to some that the Navajo were anxious to defend their country because, for nearly a century, the tribe had been treated very badly by the U.S. government.

The Navajo had lived in the American Southwest for many centuries before they first had contact with the *biligaana* (their name for white people). The two groups coexisted peacefully for a while, but by the 1840s they were at war. In 1863, the U.S. military sent Col. Kit Carson to drive the Navajo from their Arizona homes to a camp in eastern New Mexico. This brutal 350-mile (560-km) march is today remembered bitterly as "The Long Walk." After four years they were finally allowed to return—to flattened homes and burned crops.

In 1941, life on the Navajo reservation was still hard. There was no electricity, no phones, no plumbing; the small houses, called hogans, were heated by wood or coal. There were few paved roads and only a few schools. The land (some 25,000 square miles [40,000 sq km]) given to them by the United States was semidesert and not good for farming.

As a final insult, American Indians were not even allowed to vote in Arizona or New Mexico! But when they

Life was hard on the reservation. The land was dry
and rocky, terrible for growing crops. The Navajos
lived in simple dirt homes (background) called hogans.

heard the call to arms, these brave people—grandchildren of the "Long Walk" marchers—signed up to defend their government. Eighty years before, they had been fighting against the United States; now they were volunteering to fight *for* their country.

Many miles away, a white man was also figuring out a way to help his country. His idea would change the lives of the *Dine* forever.

The man's name was Philip Johnston. Though he lived in Los Angeles, where he worked as a civil engineer, he probably knew more about the Navajo than any other *biligaana* in the world. His parents had been Protestant missionaries to the Navajo. Philip moved to the reservation when he was four and spent most of his childhood there. He picked up the Navajo language at a very early age, becoming one of the few whites who could speak it well. When he was nine, he traveled to Washington, D.C., to translate for a group of Navajo leaders who were meeting with President Theodore Roosevelt.

When Johnston grew up he left the reservation and served with U.S. forces in France during World War I. By 1942, he was too old to fight again, but he still wanted to aid his country's war effort.

One day he read a newspaper story about an army unit that was experimenting with codes in American Indian languages. An idea clicked in Johnston's head: *why not the Navajo language?* Early in 1942 he went to Camp Elliott, near San Diego, to pitch his idea to the U.S. Marine Corps. He met with top officers and told them why Navajo would make an unbreakable code.

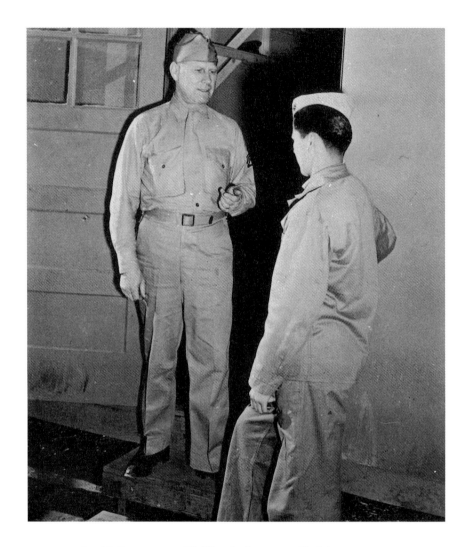

**Staff Sergeant Philip Johnston (left) grew up on a Navajo reservation. When his country entered World War II, Johnston devised an unbreakable code using the Navajo language.**

First, it was a complete mystery to the enemy. In 1941, there were only twenty-eight people outside the tribe who could speak the language—and none was German or Japanese. (Some German students had studied Indian languages in the United States before the war, but never Navajo.) And, because Navajo was an "oral language"—spoken, not written—there were no books for the enemy to study.

Second, Navajo is difficult to master. Every syllable has to be spoken exactly right; changing the pronunciation of a word can change the meaning, too. So, even if German or Japanese soldiers *did* learn the language, they could never reproduce the sounds exactly like a native.

Finally, Johnston explained, the Navajo tribe was the biggest in the United States, with more than fifty-five thousand members. It would not be hard to find men of military age who could speak both Navajo and English.

The marines weren't sure. They knew the World War I Code Talkers were used only occasionally because they didn't have words to represent all the military equipment. Aha, said Johnston. According to his plan, the Navajo wouldn't just translate messages; they would create a *code* from their language. They would invent new words, or combine existing words, for these military terms.

The marines still had doubts. So Johnston set up a demonstration on February 28, 1942. He brought four Navajos to Camp Elliott, where he sent them into separate rooms. For fifteen minutes they talked by radio, translating messages from English to Navajo and back to

As chairman of the Navajo Tribal Council, Chee Dodge (left, with son Tom) helped marine recruiters find young men to serve as Code Talkers.

English. The marines couldn't believe their eyes and ears. The Navajo system was far faster than any they'd seen.

The marines decided to recruit thirty Navajos for a "pilot program." Johnston was placed in charge of the training program. And so the Navajo Code Talkers were born.

Marine recruiters needed to find men who were fluent in both Navajo and English. So they set up shop at government-run schools, where English was taught. At first, some of the Navajos were unsure about fighting the white man's war. But when Chee Dodge, chairman of the Tribal Council, sent out a call for recruits, there was a long line of volunteers.

Some of these volunteers were so eager to serve that they lied about their age. William Dean Wilson, who was only fifteen—three years too young—changed his application when no one was looking. Others, who were too light for the 122-pound (55-kg) weight minimum, ate bunches of bananas or drank gallons of water so they would qualify.

The twenty-nine men selected for the pilot program didn't know what they were getting into. Some heard the word *marine* and confused it with *submarine*. They thought they'd be working underwater. In fact, most of the Navajos had never even seen an ocean. Little did they know that they'd soon be fighting a brutal war in the middle of the Pacific, thousands of miles from home.

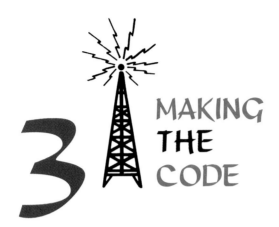

# 3 MAKING THE CODE

$F$ew of the young Navajos who traveled to basic training near San Diego had ever left the reservation before. They'd had very little contact with the *biligaana* world. So it wasn't easy for them to adapt to marine boot camp, which is grueling no matter where you come from.

Things many recruits take for granted, such as bunk beds, came as a complete surprise to the Navajo. They were baffled as well by some of the mechanical equipment and the mess-hall food. Still, they learned to adjust. One Navajo, Jimmy King, even translated the Marine Hymn into Navajo and sang it for his fellow soldiers.

One thing the Navajo *were* used to was hard work under harsh conditions. Life on the reservation had made them tough; they thought nothing of walking miles every

During their basic training in San Diego, the Code Talkers learned how to use rifles and other tools of the military trade.

day in the hot, dusty desert. So, while other soldiers complained about long hikes and heavy packs, the Navajos marched along without a word. One general said they were "without peer" when it came to physical endurance.

During one exercise, the soldiers were told to cross a desert—a two-day march—with only one canteen. On day one, while the thirsty soldiers were drinking all their water, the Navajos cut the top off a prickly pear cactus and sucked out the liquid. On day two, while others collapsed in the heat, the Navajos still had full canteens. They walked into camp while the *biligaana* soldiers rode back in a truck.

After basic training, the Code Talkers moved to California's Camp Elliott, where they learned the tools of the communications trade, such as Morse code, wire laying, pole climbing, and radio repair. Then they tackled their most important task—making an unbreakable code.

They were given a list of 211 military terms that would be needed in the field. Their job: thinking up Navajo equivalents. These words could not sound alike, because the same Navajo word pronounced three different ways might have three different meanings. Also, the words had to be easy to memorize. There would be no codebooks on the front line; the enemy must never learn the code's secrets.

On the reservation, Navajos had never come into contact with war machines. So for many code words they turned to something they did know—nature. Airplanes were named after birds. A dive bomber swooped like a

Basic training was hard work, but there was also time for play. Here three Navajos relax with a dog that adopted them during their stay at Camp Elliott.

Does this look like a fish to you? The Code Talkers named
ships after various sea creatures. A battleship was a
whale, while a destroyer was called a shark.

sparrow hawk, so it was called *gini*. Observation planes were curious, like owls (*neasjah*); torpedoes were small and fast, like swallows (*taschizzie*); bombs resembled eggs (*a-ye-shi*). Likewise, many ships were named for sea animals. A battleship was a whale (*lotso*), a destroyer a shark (*calo*), and a submarine an iron fish (*beshlo*).

The code makers came up with some colorful translations for deadly war machines. Grenades were "potatoes," mortars were "guns that squat." Their expression for bombardment was "iron rain." Later in the war (the code was expanded in 1943, 1944, and 1945), the Navajos created some equally strong words for the enemy: the Japanese were "slant eyes" (*bi-nah-ali-tsosi*). As for their side, the word for America was "Our Mother."

To spell out proper names and other words not covered in the list of 211, the Navajo created a simple alphabet code. Each letter was given a corresponding English word; that word was then translated into Navajo. Thus, instead of saying "Arizona," the code talkers would spell out the Navajo words for *a*nt *r*abbit *i*ce *z*inc *o*wl *n*ut *a*nt.

The Navajo were given only a few weeks to make the code; they often worked long into the night. When they were finished, the marines tested the code in pretend battles. For three weeks their best intelligence officers listened to the messages and tried to crack the code. They were baffled. Said one, "It sounded like gibberish. We couldn't even transcribe it, much less crack it."

The marines found some Navajo soldiers who didn't know the code and had them listen, too. They were equally confused. How could they possibly have known

Code Talkers on the island called Peleliu. Sons of the dry and dusty reservation, they were not used to the wet and steamy conditions of the South Pacific.

that "Send sparrow hawks to attack slant eye guns that squat at *sheep ant ice pig ant nut*" really meant "Send dive bombers to destroy Japanese mortars at Saipan"?

The marines were excited about their new secret weapon and anxious to put the code into action. They placed Philip Johnston in charge of training and sent two of the original Code Talkers back to the reservation to find more volunteers. (Navajos already serving in other military branches were also recruited to learn the code.)

The remaining Code Talkers were put on a boat and sent off to the South Pacific. Very soon these sons of the reservation would be fighting for their lives on an island far, far from home.

# 4 THE CODE TALKERS HIT THE BEACH

Just after bombing Pearl Harbor, Japanese troops started to invade the islands that dot the Pacific Ocean. Soon they ruled the Pacific from Japan to Australia. To win the war, the United States had to take back this territory. And so, in August 1942, marines invaded the Solomon Islands.

On the boat headed for an island called Guadalcanal (part of the Solomons island chain) was the first group of Code Talkers to see action. They were sorely needed. The U.S. troops, outmanned and outgunned by the Japanese, would need the element of surprise to win the war in the Pacific. Radio communications had to be kept absolutely secure.

Before landing on the Guadalcanal beach, the Code Talkers gave their code another test. The message they sent was a fitting one: "May the Navajo nation endure for all time to come."

U.S. soldiers storm the beach at Guadalcanal in August of 1942. During the six months of fighting that followed, the Code Talkers made sure all communications were safe and secure.

For men who grew up in the high desert of the south-western United States, Guadalcanal—like all of the Pacific islands—was a horrible place to fight. It was hot, steamy, and soaked by constant rain. Grass grew 4 or 5 feet (1.25 or 1.5 m) tall, making it hard to see the enemy or the booby traps they set. The rivers were swimming with leeches and crocodiles; the jungle floor was crawling with poisonous spiders, scorpions, snakes, and giant lizards.

The swampy ground was especially hard on the Code Talkers, who had to carry 80-pound (36-kg) radio sets through the muck. But, as they did in boot camp, they adjusted to harsh conditions quicker than their *biligaana* comrades. They knew how to live off the land; when food ran low they'd grab their slingshots, kill a stray chicken, and make stew.

Assigned to four different regiments, the Code Talkers fanned out across Guadalcanal. At first, however, they met with resistance—from their own troops. The new code seemed so simple, and so fast, that marine officers didn't trust it. One colonel set up a "race" between the Navajos and the old system, which was a machine that used rotating cylinders to turn a message into code. The Navajos were able to encode the message, send it to four different units, and receive an answer in minutes, before the mechanical device could even finish the first step.

Another colonel used his Code Talkers right away. But *biligaana* soldiers heard the strange sounds coming through the air and were frightened. They thought the Japanese had taken control of American radios. After the

At first, marine officers weren't sure how to use the Code Talkers, so they assigned them to other tasks. Here, two Navajos take their turn on observation duty.

confusion died down, one officer said the Code Talkers were "more trouble than they were worth."

Other commanders didn't understand what role the Code Talkers were supposed to play. They made them carry messages by hand or serve as ordinary fighting men. In this role, the Navajos received much praise. Accustomed to the dark desert, they were very good at night scouting. They also knew how to walk silently and keep out of the enemy's sight. Said one sergeant, "They could crawl through the jungle without a sound and hide where there wasn't anywhere to hide."

As the Pacific war raged on, the marines started to realize how fast and efficient the Code Talkers were. The leader of American forces on Guadalcanal asked for eighty-three more Code Talkers at the end of 1942.

In 1943, the U.S. Navy asked to "borrow" some Code Talkers, too. They had been trying to destroy Japanese forces on an island called Rabaul. But whenever they tried, the Japanese, who had intercepted and cracked the navy's code, were waiting to shoot U.S. planes out of the sky. With the Code Talkers in charge of communications, however, American planes sneaked in undetected. The attack was a success.

As U.S. forces swept north, knocking the Japanese out of the Pacific islands, the Code Talkers proved to be very valuable. They provided a link between headquarters and the front line. If the front line needed reinforcements, ammunition, or medical help, the Code Talkers could send the message. If they knew where enemy forces were located, they could help the U.S. artillery soldiers aim their

Used to traveling about their reservation in the
dark, the Navajos proved to be very good at night
scouting. One sergeant said they could "hide
where there wasn't anywhere to hide."

guns. They could also redirect those guns if "friendly fire" was landing on American forces.

Obviously, this was very tense work. One small mistake in translation and the Code Talkers might send hundreds of marines to their deaths.

Death is a constant fear for men and women in battle. For the Code Talkers, though, it was an even graver concern. The Navajo believe that living people can be hurt by spirits of the dead (unless they're protected by a religious ceremony). These spirits, called *chindi*, remain on earth after a person dies, terrorizing anyone who comes near the corpse.

The war in the Pacific was an especially bloody one. *Chindi* were everywhere. Many Code Talkers later reported that they had a hard time dealing with all the dead bodies. But this fear did not keep them from fulfilling their duties.

Throughout the war, the Navajo soldiers received comfort and hope from their religious customs and beliefs. For protection, most carried buckskin pouches filled with corn pollen (corn is a sacred plant for the Navajo people). Some also carried medicine made from the gallbladders of skunks, bears, eagles, and mountain lions. This was thought to guard them from strangers. One Code Talker said he never sent a message without asking the Spirit to help him.

Back on the reservation, the families of the Code Talkers also asked the Spirit to protect their men. The mother of one soldier went to a sacred hill every morning to pray with her corn pollen. Other relatives planted

On Okinawa, a Navajo marine beats out a rhythm on a native drum. The Code Talkers brought many of their customs and traditions from the Arizona reservation to the Pacific islands.

"prayer feathers"—feathers decorated with turquoise—in the desert.

In 1944, the tribe held a special ceremony for all the Navajos in the Pacific, who were represented by photographs. This ceremony was meant to protect the Code Talkers from the *chindi* of the enemies they had killed.

# 5 BAFFLING THE ENEMY

The Japanese were completely baffled by the Navajo code. One Code Talker recalls that sometimes, when he was broadcasting a message, a Japanese radio operator would come onto his frequency and ask (in English), "Who's this?" The Code Talker simply laughed and told the Japanese to get lost.

The Americans, on the other hand, were thrilled by the code's success. For speed and accuracy, the Navajos couldn't be beat. And so, as the Marines pushed north toward Japan—moving from island to island—two Code Talkers were assigned to every battalion. (It was found that friends or cousins made the best pairs, because they would practice while off-duty.)

Though the code was a hit, it still needed some tinkering. New weapons, planes, and ships were constantly

Because of their dark skin and hair, the Navajos
were sometimes mistaken for Japanese soldiers.
This made life very dangerous for the Code Talkers.

being invented; code words were needed for things like bazookas. By 1943, approximately 200 terms had been added to the original 211. Every few months the Code Talkers would gather in Hawaii to learn and practice these additions.

When the marines hit a beach, the Code Talkers were often among the first ones off the boat. They would set up a tall antenna, then tie the generator to a coconut tree. The words *New Mexico* or *Arizona* crackling across their receivers signaled that a message was about to be sent in Navajo code.

Like most soldiers, the Code Talkers—especially those on the front lines—were faced with constant danger. Sometimes the danger came from their own countrymen. In the heat of battle, *biligaana* soldiers couldn't always tell a Navajo from a Japanese. They did, in fact, share similar features: dark hair, dark skin, high cheekbones. Also, the Japanese sometimes took uniforms from dead GIs and tried to sneak across U.S. lines.

This made U.S. soldiers very jumpy and made things very risky for the American Indians. One Code Talker was taken prisoner by the U.S. Army while looking for orange juice in a mess tent. Before he convinced his captors to take him back to his unit, where he was identified, they talked about shooting him. Another Code Talker was "skinny-dipping" (swimming naked) when the military police captured him at gunpoint. If a Navajo buddy hadn't recognized him, he too might have been shot. After close calls like these, some units assigned a bodyguard to each Code Talker.

Most of the *biligaana* were happy to serve as body-guards, because they knew how much they owed to the Code Talkers. Here is just one example of that debt. On the island of Guam, American scouts discovered that the Japanese were preparing to attack a unit of marines. A Code Talker quickly relayed this message to HQ, along with the enemy's location. Two artillery units were able to wipe out the Japanese forces, thus saving the marines on the front line.

As the American "island hopping" campaign continued, the Code Talkers approached the scene of their greatest triumph—the Battle of Iwo Jima. Iwo Jima was nothing to look at—a rocky little bump in the Pacific, only 5 miles (8 km) long, with an extinct volcano at one end. It also wasn't much to smell, thanks to the stinky sulfur springs (Iwo Jima means "Sulfur Island"). Because it was close to Japan, however, the island was very important to both sides. The United States needed it as a base for fighter planes to attack the Japanese mainland. They would do anything to take Iwo Jima.

In February 1945, a huge force of marines sailed for Iwo Jima. As they approached, some of the Code Talkers reached for their pouches of corn pollen. They knew they had a dangerous task before them. The island was defended by twenty-two thousand Japanese who were ready to die in service to their country.

When they landed, the Code Talkers set up shop on the beach. They had never worked in more dangerous conditions; bullets whistled overhead, and mortar shells blew huge holes in the beach. They also had never

On the island of Guam, two Navajo
marines wait for battle. The Navajos
saved many American lives on Guam
with their uncrackable code.

When American marines raised the flag on Iwo Jima's Mount Suribachi, it was the Code Talkers who spread the news. (Ira Hayes, one of the soldiers pictured, was a Pima Indian.)

worked harder. During the first forty-eight hours, six Navajo radio units toiled around the clock. One officer estimated that they sent eight hundred messages during those two days—"without error."

The battle raged on until the morning of February 23, when six U.S. soldiers raised the flag on top of the volcano. From the front line, the message came like this: "*Naastsosi thanzie dibeh shida dahnestsa tkin shush wollachee moasi lin achi.*" A Code Talker translated: *Mouse turkey sheep uncle ram ice bear ant cat horse intestines.* Everybody at HQ knew what those words meant. American forces had finally taken Mt. Suribachi. The Battle of Iwo Jima was almost over.

Three Code Talkers were killed and many more wounded on Iwo Jima. But their suffering was not in vain. Maj. Howard Conner, signal officer of the Fifth Marine Division, said, "Were it not for the Navajo Code Talkers, the marines never would have taken Iwo Jima."

The marines' final stop in the Pacific was Okinawa, an island less than 400 miles (640 km) from Japan. Again the Code Talkers served. In fact, a Code Talker was working the radio on August 10, 1945, when he received an

**The Code Talkers served proudly on many Pacific islands—including Saipan, pictured here—but they were surely glad to return to their homes on the reservation.**

urgent message—the Japanese had surrendered. World War II was finally over.

From Rabaul to Iwo Jima, the Code Talkers played an important role. They served in all six Marine Corps divisions in the Pacific. Besides the islands already mentioned—Saipan, Guam, Okinawa—they also fought on New Britain, Bougainville, Tarawa, Peleliu, and others. Eleven Code Talkers died in service to the United States, "Our Mother." The rest returned to their own nation in the Arizona desert, glad to see the last of history's bloodiest war.

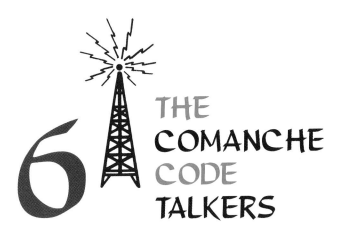

# 6 THE COMANCHE CODE TALKERS

Code Talkers were not the only Navajos to participate in World War II. About thirty-six hundred Navajos served on all fronts. Others helped the war effort at home, working in weapons factories and growing food for the troops.

Nor was theirs the only American Indian tribe to fight. Nearly twenty-five thousand American Indians enlisted in the U.S. armed services during the war. Perhaps the most famous was Ira Hayes. This Pima Indian was one of six marines who raised the American flag on Iwo Jima's Mt. Suribachi.

Though they haven't received as much attention, other American Indians also worked as coders in World War II. In Africa, Italy, and the Pacific, members of various tribes—Creek, Menominee, Ojibwa, and Hopi—were hired to speak on all fronts. The Choctaws, who helped develop Code Talking during World War I, also returned. Unlike the Navajos, however, these groups did not create an extensive code; they simply sent messages in their native tongue. Often this was enough to fool the enemy.

The Comanches, from southwestern Oklahoma, were also recruited for their language skills. Their language was unwritten and mostly unknown to whites, and therefore perfect for secret communications.

Most of the Comanche recruits came from government-run boarding schools. This is ironic. In these schools the Comanches were taught to speak nothing but English. One Comanche, Roderick "Dick" Red Elk, remembers hearing as a boy that he shouldn't bother with his native tongue because there was no future in it. In fact, he was punished at school for speaking Comanche. Luckily for the U.S. military, Red Elk and his friends didn't listen and became fluent in both languages.

Eighteen Comanches enlisted as signalmen. After learning the basics of telephone and radio operations at Fort Benning, Georgia, they shipped out for Europe in 1942 as members of the U.S. Army's 4th Signal Company of the 4th Infantry Division.

In England, the Comanches agreed on certain military code words. Their list, though not as long as the Navajo's four-hundred-word code, served its purpose. Tanks were called "turtles" (*wah-cah-tay*), because both have hard shells. The Comanches have only one word for gun, so they added descriptive words at the beginning. A machine gun, for example, was called a "sewing-machine

During "maneuvers" (practice battles) in Tennessee, a Hopi Indian talks to a fellow tribesman in their native tongue. Members of many tribes served as Code Talkers in World War II.

gun," because both make *rat-a-tat* sounds. They also have just one word for airplane, so they distinguished a bomber by calling it a "pregnant airplane"!

On June 6, 1944—a date known as "D-Day"—fourteen Comanche Code Talkers were part of the greatest invasion in military history. With the 4th Infantry, they landed on Utah Beach at Normandy. Their goal: driving German soldiers out of France. (They had practiced for this battle in the English Channel, "invading" the British coast.)

The Comanches hit the sand running, climbing 20-foot (6-m) poles to string communications lines while dodging German bullets. They helped the 4th Infantry make a smooth landing on Utah Beach, sending messages back to headquarters about the enemy's strengths and weaknesses.

After the Normandy invasion, the Comanches participated in battles in northern France and Luxembourg that pushed the Germans back across their border. They helped defeat the Nazis at St. Lo, and played a part in the Battle of the Bulge.

The Comanche Code Talkers fought with words as well as with guns. At all times they fought bravely. Two were wounded in action; one was awarded the Bronze Star for his heroism in fighting the Nazis.

# 7 BACK TO THE RESERVATION

When they got back to the reservation, the American Indian veterans tried to forget about the war. Some returned to their jobs; the boys who lied about their age to enlist went back to school. For others, the adjustment was not so easy. They had nightmares about their horrible experiences across the ocean.

Again, the Navajos turned to their religion for support. Many of the returning Code Talkers participated in a ceremony called "The Enemy Way." As part of this three-day ritual, a medicine man took an object related to the enemy—maybe a weapon or piece of clothing taken from a Japanese victim—and buried it in the ground. This helped to cleanse the Navajo of their bad memories.

The bad experiences weren't all left overseas. Life on the reservation was still hard. Treated as equals in the

A Navajo medicine man practices his art. When the
Code Talkers returned from battle, medicine men
helped them to get rid of their bad memories.

Peter MacDonald speaks during the Navajo Code Talkers Day celebration. Some forty years earlier, MacDonald had served as a Code Talker; he was later elected chairman of the tribe.

marines, some Code Talkers returned to states where they weren't even allowed to vote. Jobs were still hard to come by; the land was still poor; people still went hungry.

In many ways, however, World War II changed reservation life for the better. Seeing how education had helped the Code Talkers—and the *biligaana* soldiers they fought alongside—Navajo children started attending school in greater numbers. For the men who fought, seeing the world beyond the reservation gave them the urge to make things better for their people. They took an active role in leading their tribes. In 1970, Peter MacDonald and Wilson Skeet—two former Code Talkers—were elected chairman and vice chairman of the Navajo Nation.

Sadly, for many years the heroic deeds of the Code Talkers went unrecognized in the *biligaana* world (except for a few scattered newspaper and magazine articles). The marines wanted to keep the code under wraps, in case it might be needed in future wars. So the American Indian vets were asked not to speak publicly about their work.

In 1968, however, the code was "declassified" (made public). And once the word was out, the world was fascinated by America's secret weapon in the war.

In 1969, some twenty-five years after the fighting had stopped, the Navajo Code Talkers were honored at a reunion of the 4th Marine Division Association. This ceremony was reported in all the nation's newspapers. In 1971, the Code Talkers held their own reunion at Window Rock, Arizona. Also in 1971, U.S. president Richard Nixon awarded the Navajos a certificate praising their "patriotism, resourcefulness, and courage."

On July 28, 1982, President Ronald Reagan signed a motion naming August 14 "National Navajo Code Talkers Day." Arizona senator Dennis DeConcini explained why he sponsored the motion. "Since the Code Talkers' work required absolute secrecy," he said, "they never enjoyed

In 1989—more than four decades after serving their country in faraway lands—the Navajo Code Talkers proudly display the symbols of their accomplishments.

General Colin Powell (right) joins
Navajo Code Talkers and their families
as they inspect the Pentagon exhibit
that honors their brave deeds.

the national acclaim they so much deserved. I do not want this illustrious yet unassuming group of Navajo marines to fade into history without notice."

The Comanche and Choctaw Code Talkers were noticed, too. At a 1989 ceremony in Oklahoma, the surviving soldiers were decorated by the French government for their work in helping drive the Nazis out of France. The French also gave "Knight of the National Order of Merit" medals to the Comanche and Choctaw nations.

In 1992, exactly fifty years after the first Code Talkers were recruited, a group of Navajos traveled to Washington, D.C., to dedicate a temporary exhibit about the Code Talkers at the Pentagon (U.S. military headquarters). They translated a prayer for peace that was phoned in by a Navajo in Arizona. The code still worked! Then Arizona senator John McCain spoke about the Code Talkers: "Their courage, resourcefulness, and tenacity saved the lives of countless men and women."

On the other side of the world, one more tribute was paid to the Code Talkers. Many years after the war, a Japanese general was told that the U.S. Marines had used a code based on an American Indian language. "Thank you," he said, relieved. "That is a puzzle I thought would never be solved." That unsolvable puzzle was one of the great stories of World War II—a story that deserves to be remembered by generations to come.

# FOR FURTHER READING

Aaseng, Nathan. *Navajo Code Talkers*. New York: Walker, 1992.

Doherty, Craig A. and Katherine M. Doherty. *The Apaches and Navajos*. New York: Franklin Watts, 1989.

Katz, William Loren. *World War II to the New Frontier, 1940–1963*. Austin, Tex.: Raintree Steck-Vaughn, 1993.

Lewis, Shari. *Secrets, Signs, Signals & Codes*. New York: Holt, Rinehart and Winston, 1980.

Mango, Karin N. *Codes, Ciphers, and Other Secrets*. New York: Franklin Watts, 1988.

Wood, Leigh Hope. *The Navajo Indians*. New York: Chelsea House, 1991.

Wright, David K. *A Multicultural Portrait of World War II*. New York: Marshall Cavendish, 1994.

# INDEX

# ABOUT THE AUTHOR

Robert Daily received a B.A. in English literature from Carleton College and a master's degree in English literature from the University of Chicago. He is a magazine writer for both adults and children and is also the author of *Earth*, *Mercury*, *Sun*, and *Pluto* in the First Book series. He lives with his wife, Janet, in Chicago.

DISCARD